Little Mitchie

SELF-DRIVING CARS

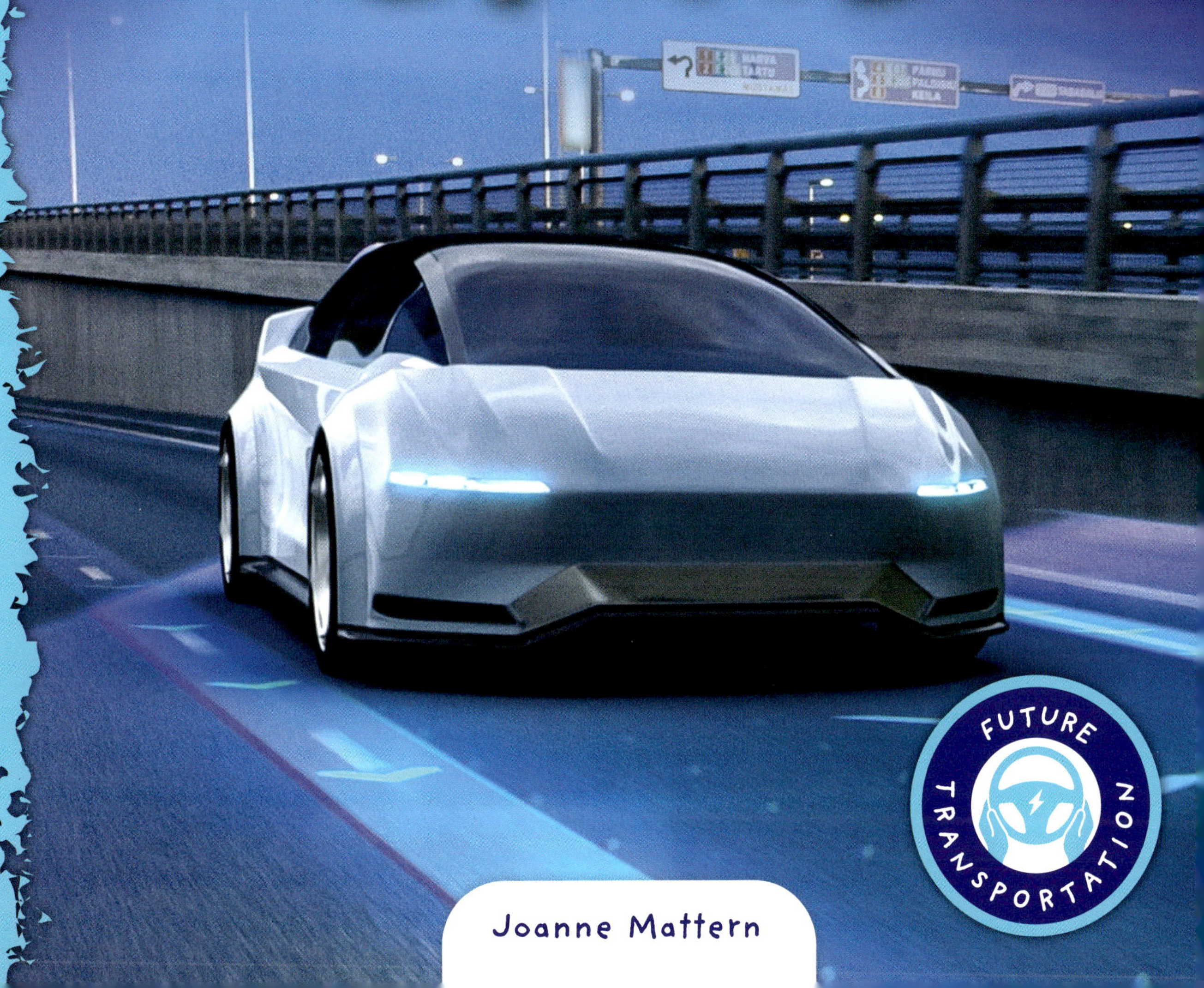

Joanne Mattern

CREATING YOUNG NONFICTION READERS

Little Mitchie books spark curiosity and support early nonfiction reading for students in Grades 2-3. Designed to build vocabulary, support second language learners, and prepare readers for middle-grade content, each book includes helpful tips for parents and educators to build confidence and deepen understanding of the world.

TIPS FOR READING NONFICTION WITH BEGINNING READERS

Talk about Nonfiction

Begin by explaining that nonfiction books give us information that is true. The book will be organized around a specific topic or idea, and we may learn new facts through reading.

Look at the Parts

Most nonfiction books have helpful features. Our *Little Mitchie* titles include color photographs and graphic aids, a table of contents, a glossary, and an index. Share the purpose of these features with your reader.

Color Photos and Graphic Aids

A lot of information can be found by "reading" photos, charts, maps, and other graphic aids found within nonfiction texts. Help your reader learn more about the different ways information can be displayed.

Table of Contents

Located at the front of the book, this list shows the big ideas within the text and the page numbers where they can be found.

Glossary

Located at the back of the book, the glossary defines key words and phrases that are related to the topic. These words and phrases can be found in the text in colored type.

Index

Located at the back of the book, an index is an alphabetical list of topics and the page numbers where they can be found.

With a little help and guidance about reading nonfiction, you can feel good about introducing a young reader to the world of *Little Mitchie* nonfiction books.

Little Mitchie is an imprint of:

Mitchell Lane
PUBLISHERS

2001 SW 31st Avenue
Hallandale, FL 33009
mitchelllanepub.com

First Edition, 2027.

Author: Joanne Mattern
Designer: Bobbie Houser
Editor: Tricia Hoffman

Library of Congress Cataloging-in-Publication Data
Title: Self-Driving Cars / by Joanne Mattern

Description: Hallandale, FL :
Mitchell Lane Publishers, [2027]

Identifiers:
ISBN 979-8-89260-866-4 (library bound)
ISBN 979-8-89260-963-0 (eBook)

Library of Congress Control Number: 2026936194

PHOTO CREDITS
Alamy: Sueddeutsche Zeitung Photo, 10; Malcolm Park, 11; Zuma Press, Inc., 13; Shutterstock: Gorodenkoff, cover, 1, 5, 19, 20, 21; bluestork, 7; Kinwunz, 9; Iv-olga, 14, 22; Scharfsinn, 17; Sundry Photography, 22.

TABLE OF CONTENTS

Chapter One

WHO IS DRIVING?

Maya watched from the curb as a car pulled up beside her. She got into the backseat.

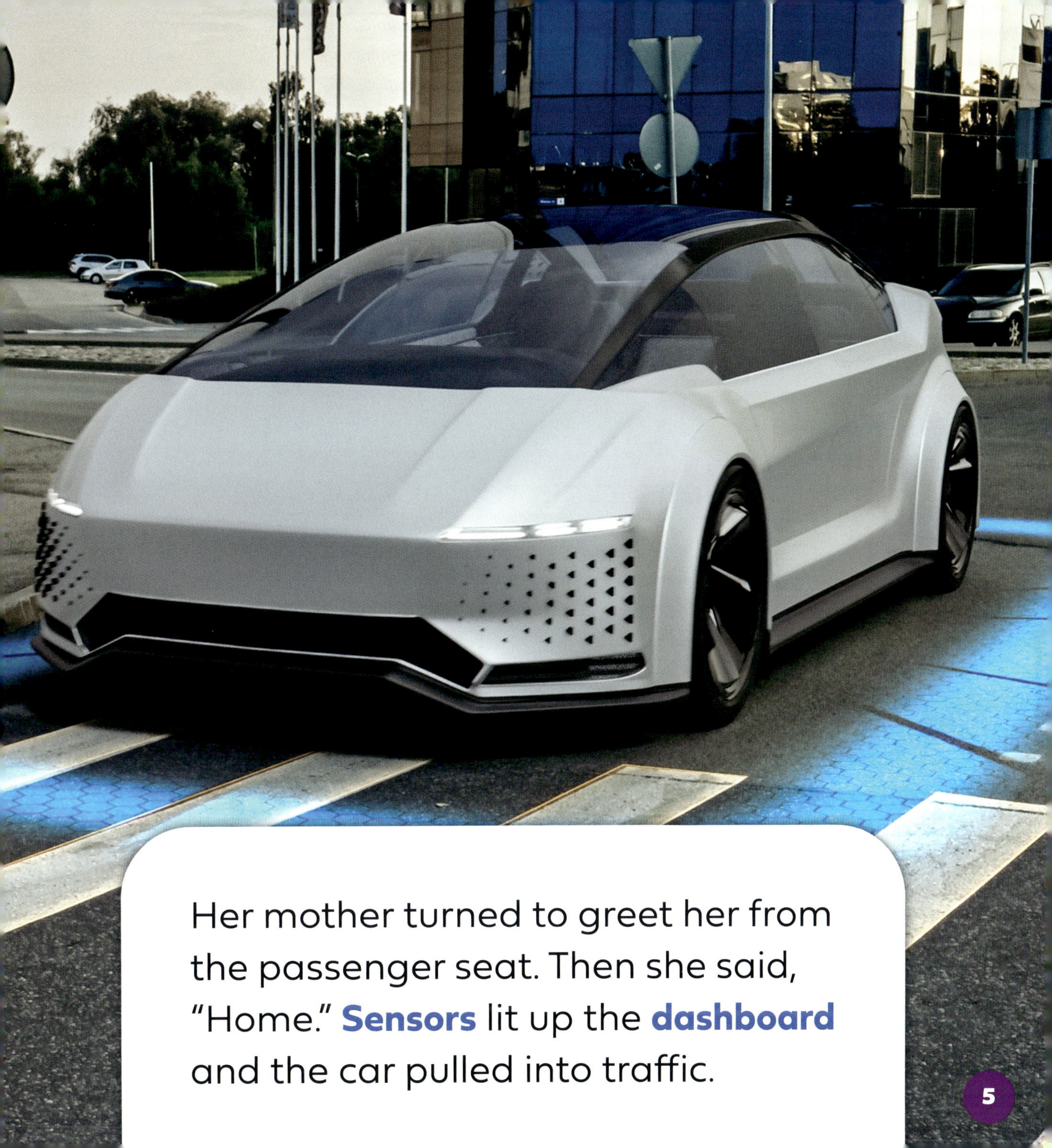

Her mother turned to greet her from the passenger seat. Then she said, “Home.” **Sensors** lit up the **dashboard** and the car pulled into traffic.

"It's strange to ride in a car with no driver," Maya said. She watched the steering wheel turn by itself.

The car pulled into the parking space right in front of Maya's home. Maya laughed.

"The car parks better than you do," she teased her mother.

Please keep your hands off the wheel
The Waymo Driver is in control at all times
D
13
START
STOP
A/C
69°F
AUTO
MAX
D

Chapter Two

SELF-DRIVING CARS TODAY

A self-driving car is a vehicle that can drive without a person doing the work. But how?

Cameras and sensors tell the car what is happening. **GPS** tells the car where to go. The car's computer controls the action.

A SAFER WAY TO DRIVE

Almost all car crashes are caused by humans. Self-driving cars could prevent accidents and save thousands of lives.

In 1925, a man used a radio to control a car through New York City. The car crashed, but people still liked the idea. They wanted to make driving more **automated**.

AN ANCIENT IDEA

Way back in 1478, Leonardo da Vinci built a cart that could drive itself. You could say that was the first self-driving car!

In the early 2000s, the U.S. government held a contest to see if anyone could invent a self-driving car. The car had to drive through a difficult course that resembled heavy city traffic. In 2007, six teams successfully did just that.

ON THE LEVEL

Self-driving cars are rated on a scale from zero to five. Level zero means the driver has complete control. Level five means the car doesn't need a driver at all.

Are there self-driving cars on the road today? Yes—but you can't buy one yet. They are used in other ways for now.

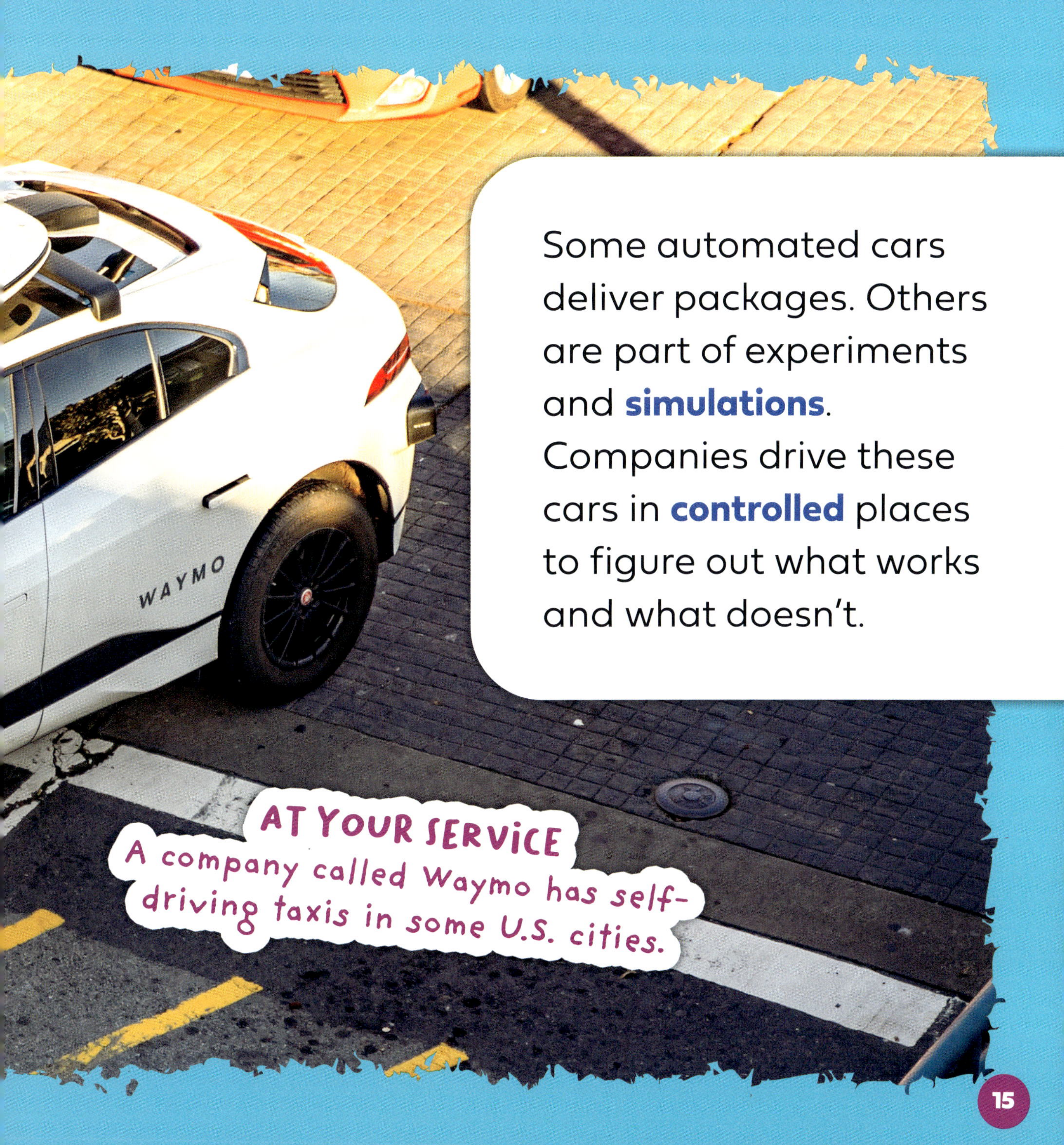

Some automated cars deliver packages. Others are part of experiments and **simulations**. Companies drive these cars in **controlled** places to figure out what works and what doesn't.

AT YOUR SERVICE

A company called Waymo has self-driving taxis in some U.S. cities.

Chapter Three

FUTURE DRIVING

Today, it is legal in some places for self-driving cars to be on the road, but a person has to be in the car and ready to drive.

WHO'S TO BLAME?
Laws make it difficult for self-driving cars. Who would be responsible in the event of an accident? The answer is complicated.

Many people think self-driving cars are a great idea. They could be safer and provide people with more free time.

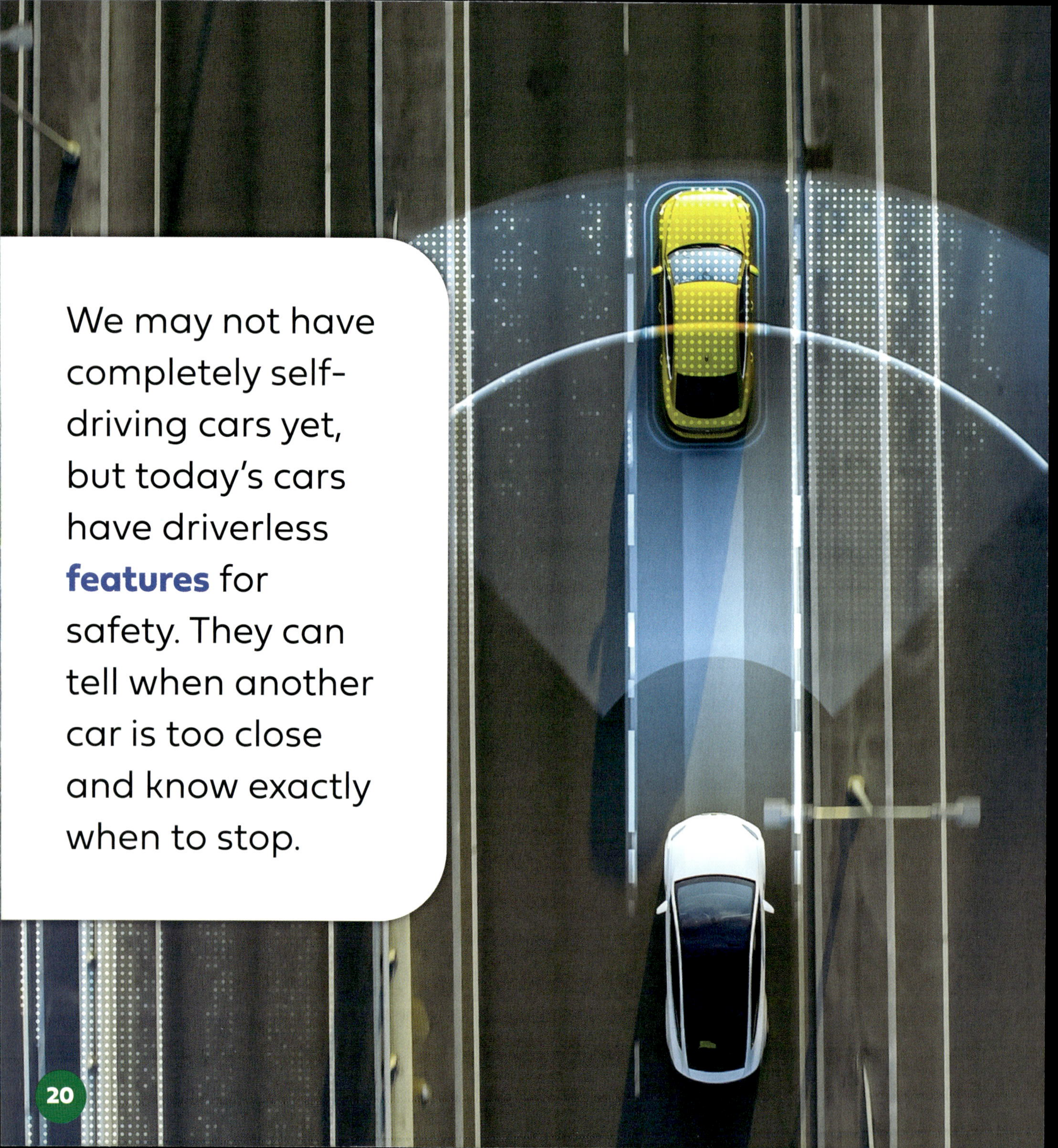

We may not have completely self-driving cars yet, but today's cars have driverless **features** for safety. They can tell when another car is too close and know exactly when to stop.

Self-driving cars will provide passengers with a fun and safe ride in the future!

LET'S LOOK AT A SELF-DRIVING CAR

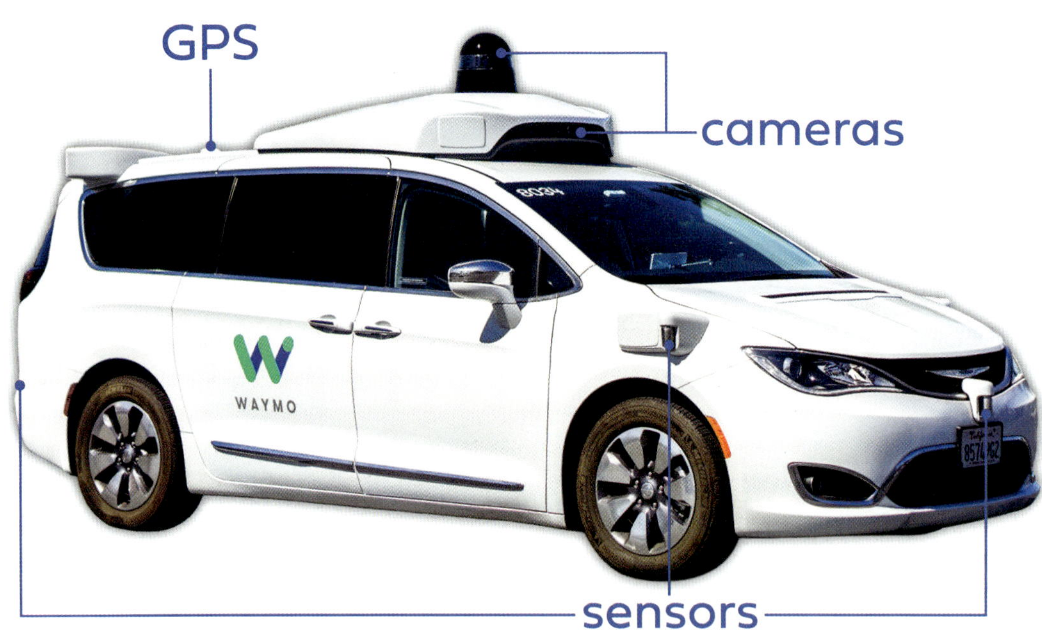

GLOSSARY

automated (aw-tuh-may-tid) operated by machines

controlled (kuhn-trold) under the direction of someone

dashboard (dash-bord) the part of a car that contains the controls

features (fee-churz) particular parts or qualities of something

GPS (gee-pee-ess) Global Positioning System; a worldwide system of maps

scale (skale) a system of measurement

sensors (sen-surz) devices that detect or measure changes and transmit information

simulations (sim-yuh-lay-shuhnz) trial runs to act out a real event

FURTHER READING

Grack, Rachel. *Automobiles from Then to Now.* Amicus Ink, 2020.

Rathburn, Betsy. *Self-Driving Cars.* Bellwether Media, 2021.

ON THE INTERNET

Driverless Car Facts for Kids
https://kids.kiddle.co/Driverless_car
Children can learn about the history of driverless cars, how they work, and what the future holds.

Driverless Cars Facts
www.softschools.com/facts/technology/driverless_cars_facts/3362/
Check out fun facts about driverless cars, how they work, and the challenges they face.

INDEX